THE ART OF TAROT CARDS

CD-ROM & BOOK

Edited by
Alan Weller

IL MATTO

DOVER PUBLICATIONS, INC.
Mineola, New York

The CD-ROM inside this book contains all of the cards from ten different tarot decks, plus the Major Arcana from the *Tarocco Italiano*. There is no installation necessary. Just insert the CD into your computer and call the images into your favorite software (refer to the documentation with your software for further instructions). Each image has been scanned at 300 dpi and saved in both 72-dpi Internet-ready and 300-dpi high-resolution JPEG format.

In order to include as many tarot decks as possible, only a selection of cards from each deck are shown in the book. The range of numbers listed at the bottom of each page indicates the entire deck. The "Images" folder on the CD contains two different folders. All of the high resolution JPEG files have been placed in one folder and all of the Internet-ready JPEG files can be found in the other folder. The images in each of these folders are identical. Within each of these two folders are eleven folders, each one containing one tarot deck.

Every image has a unique file name in the following format: xxx.xxx. The first 3 digits of the file name, before the period, correspond to the number printed with the images in the book. The last 3 letters of the file name "JPG," refer to the file format. So, 001.JPG would be the first file in the JPG folder.

Also included on the CD-ROM is Dover Design Manager, a simple graphics editing program for Windows that will allow you to view, print, crop, and rotate the images.

For technical support, contact:
Telephone: 1 (617) 249-0245
Fax: 1 (617) 249-0245
Email: dover@artimaging.com
Internet: **http://www.dovertechsupport.com**
The fastest way to receive technical support is via email or the Internet.

Copyright
Copyright © 2010 by Dover Publications, Inc.
Electronic images copyright © 2010 by Dover Publications, Inc.
All rights reserved.

Bibliographical Note
The Art of Tarot Cards CD-ROM & Book, is a new work, first published by Dover Publications, Inc., in 2010.

Dover Electronic Clip Art®

International Standard Book Number
ISBN-13: 978-0-486-99085-9
ISBN-10: 0-486-99085-0

Manufactured in the United States by Courier Corporation
99085001
www.doverpublications.com

LE FOU

    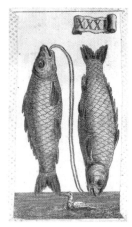

IL MATTO

IL BAGATTO

LA PAPESSA

L' IMPERATRICE

L' IMPERATORE

LA GIUSTIZIA

IL PAPA

IL CARRO

GLI AMANTI

VIIII

L' EREMITA

XIII

LA MORTE

X

LA RUOTA DELLA FORTUNA

XI

LA FORZA

XII

L' APPESO

XIV

L' INTEMPERANZA

XV

IL DIAVOLO

XVI

LA TORRE

XVIII

LA LUNA

IL MATTO

XII

L' APPESO

I

IL BAGATTEL.

LA PAPESSA

III

E IMPERATRICE

L' IMPERATORE

V

IL PAPA

VI

GLI AMANTI

VII

IL CARRO

121–198 *The Classic Tarot*

VIII

LA GIUSTIZIA

IX

L' EREMITA

X

RUOT. DELLA FOR.

XI

LA FORZA

XVII

LE STELLE

XIII

XIV

LA TEMPERAN.

XV

IL DIAVOLO

XVI

LA TORRE

XVIII

LA LUNA

XIX

IL SOLE

XX

IL GIUDIZIO

XXI

IL MONDO

121–198 *The Classic Tarot*

11

RE DI DANARI	RE DI COPPE	RE DI SPADE	RE DI BASTONI
CAVAL DI DAN.	CAVAL DI COPPE	CAVAL DI SPADI	CAV. DI BASTONI
REG. DI DANARI	REG. DI COPPE	REG. DI SPADE	REG. DI BASTONI

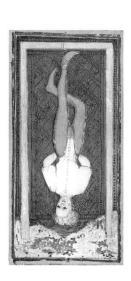

199–276 *I Tarocchi Dei Visconti*

THE FOOL .

THE MAGICIAN.

THE HIGH PRIESTESS

THE EMPRESS.

THE EMPEROR.

THE HIEROPHANT

THE LOVERS.

THE CHARIOT.

STRENGTH.

THE HERMIT.

WHEEL of FORTUNE.

JUSTICE .

THE HANGED MAN.

TEMPERANCE.

DEATH.

THE DEVIL.

THE TOWER.

THE STAR.

THE MOON.

THE SUN.

JUDGEMENT.

THE WORLD.

290–354 *The Waite-Smith Tarot*

KING of CUPS.

KING of PENTACLES.

KING of SWORDS.

KING of WANDS

KNIGHT of CUPS.

KNIGHT of PENTACLES.

KNIGHT of SWORDS.

KNIGHT of WANDS.

QUEEN of CUPS.

QUEEN of PENTACLES

QUEEN of SWORDS.

QUEEN of WANDS.

MISERO·I·

IMPERATOR·VIIII· 2

H ARTIXAN·III· 3

E· MERCHADANTE·IIII· 4

E ZINTILOMO·V· 5

E CHAVALIER·VI· 6

A· MARTE·XXXXV· 4

E· PAPA·X· 10

D CALIOPE·XI· 11

D VRANIA·XII· 12

D TERPSICORE·XIII· 13

D ERATO·XIIII· 14

MERCVRIO XXXXII · 42
VENVS XXXXIII · 43
SOL XXXXIIII · 44
IVPITER XXXXVI · 46

SATVRNO XXXXVII · 47
OCTAVA SPERA · XXXXVIII · 48
PRIMO MOBILE XXXXVIIII · 49
PRIMA CAVSA XXXXX · 50

DOXE · VII ·
TEMPERANCIA XXXIIII ·
LOICA XXII
FAMEIO II

355–404 *I Tarocchi Del Mantegna*

25

0. LE FOU ש

1 LE BATELEUR א

2 LA PAPESSE ב

3 L'IMPERATRICE ג

4 L'EMPEREUR ד

5 LE PAPE ה

6 L'AMOURAUX ו

7 LE CHARIOT ז

8 LA JUSTICE ח

9 L'ERMITE ט

10 LA ROUE DE FORTUNE י

11 LA FORCE כ

12 | LE PENDU

13 | LA MORT

14 | LA TEMPERANCE

15 | LE DIABLE

16 | LE FEU DU CIEL

17 | LES ETOILES

18 | LA LUNE

19 | LE SOLEIL

20 | LE JUDGMENT

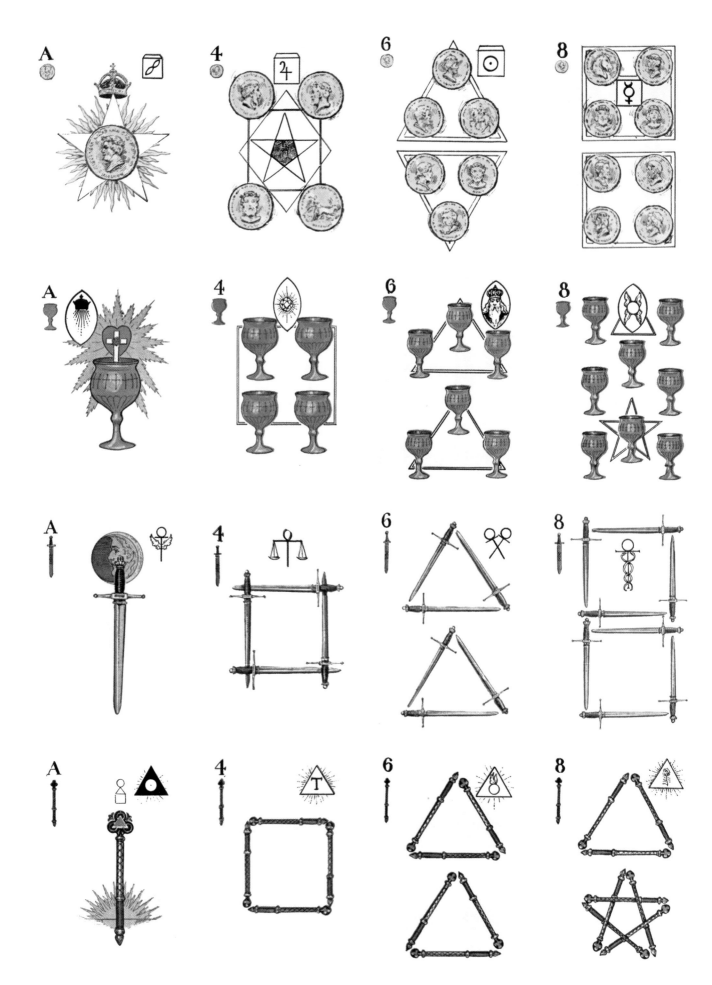

28   405–482 *The Knapp-Hall Tarot*

405–482 *The Knapp-Hall Tarot*

LE·FOL

LE·BATELEUR

·JVNON

LIMPERATRICE

LEMPEREVR

·JVPITER·

AMOVREOX

LE·CHARIOT

LA·IVSTICE

LERMITE

LAROVXDEFORTVNE

·LA·FORCE·

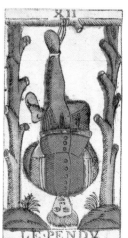

LE·PENDV

LA·MAISONDIEU

TENPERANCE

LE·DIABLE

LE·TOILLE

LA·LVNE

LE·SOLEIL

·LE·IVGEMENT

·LE·MONDE·

CHEVALIER DE DENIERS   CHEVALIER DE COUPES   CHEVALIER DESPEE   CHEVALIER DE BASTONS

REINE DE DENIERS   REINE DE COUPES   REINE DESPEE   REINE DE BASTONS

ROY DE DENIERS .   ROY DE COUPES .   ROY DESPEE   ROY DE BASTONS

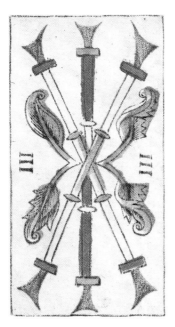
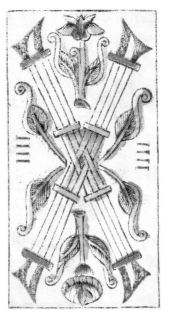
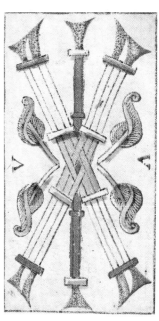

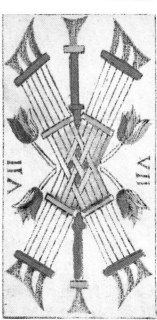
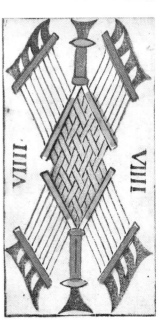

I

Il Bagattelliere

II

Là Papessa

III

L'Imperatrice

IV

L'Imperatore

V

Il Papa

Il Matto

VI

Gli Amanti

VII

Il Carro

VIII

La Giustizia

561–638 *Ancient Tarot of Lombardy*

IX

L'Eremita

X

La ruota della Fortuna

XI

La Forza

XII

L'Appeso

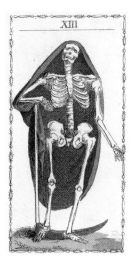

XIII

XIV

La Temperanza

XV

Il Diavolo

XVI

La Torre

XVII

Le Stelle

XVIII

La Luna

XIX

Il Sole

XX

Il Guidizio

XXI

Il Mondo

Il Re di danari Il Re di Coppe Il Re di Spade Il Re di Bastoni

Il Cavaliere di Danari Il Cavaliere di Coppe Il Cavaliere di Spade Il Cavaliere di Bastoni

Il Fante di danari Il Fante di Coppe Il Fante di Spade Il Fante di Bastoni

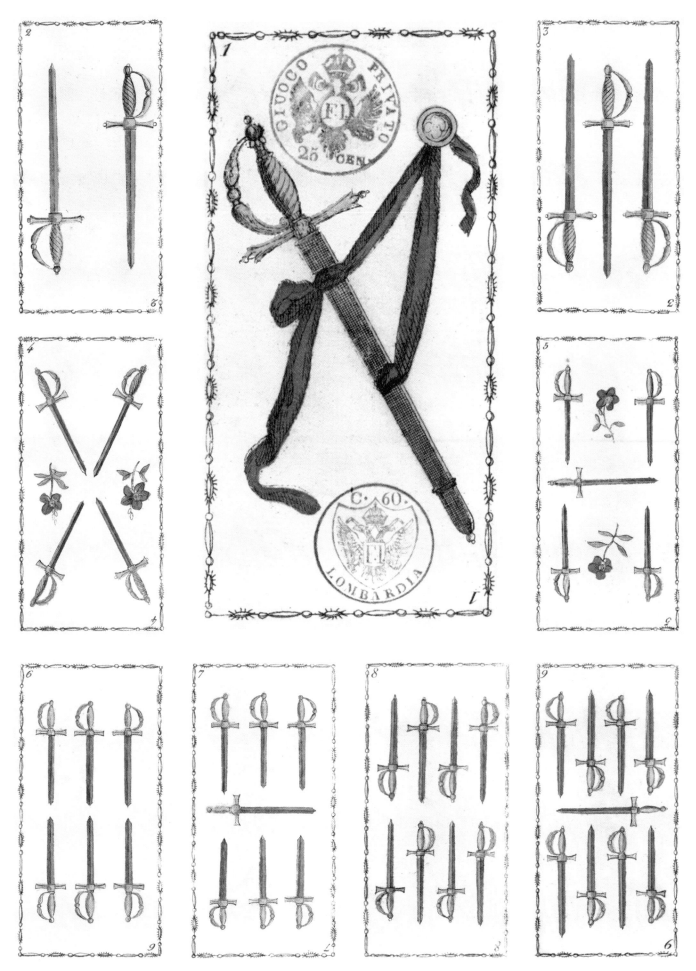

561–638 *Ancient Tarot of Lombardy* 37

I

LE BATELEVR

LE FOL

II

LA PAPESSE

III

LA IMPERATRICE

IIII

LE EMPEREVR

V

LE PAPE

VI

LAMOREVX

VII

LE CHARIOT

VIII

LA IVSTICE

VIIII

LE ERMITE

X

ROVE DE FORTVNE

XI

LA FORCE

XII

LE PENDV

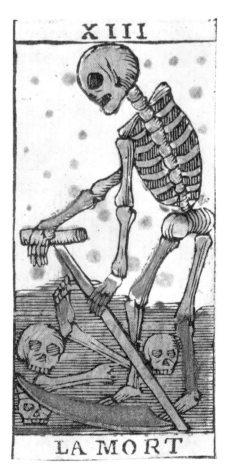

XIII

LA MORT

XIIII

LA TEMPERANCE

XV

LE DIABLE

XVI

LA MAISONDIEV

XVII

LE TOILLE

XVIII

LA LVNE

XVIIII

LE SOLE

XX

LE IVGEMENT

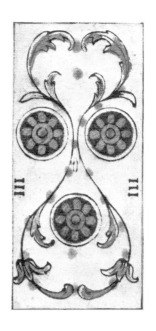

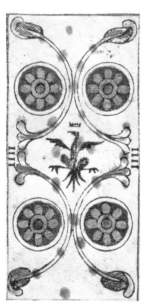

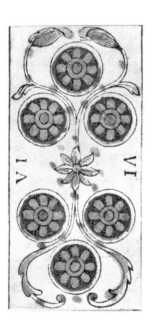

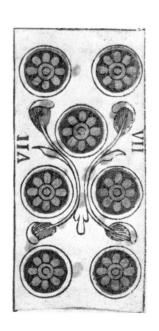

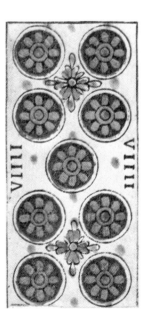

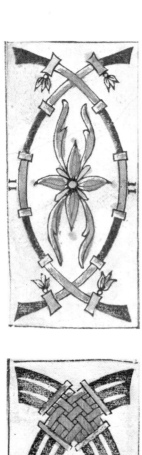
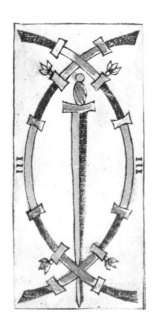
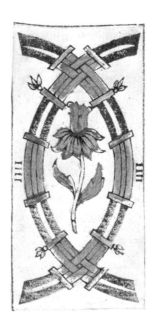
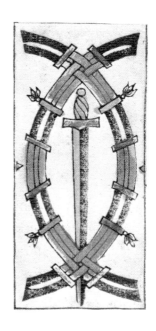

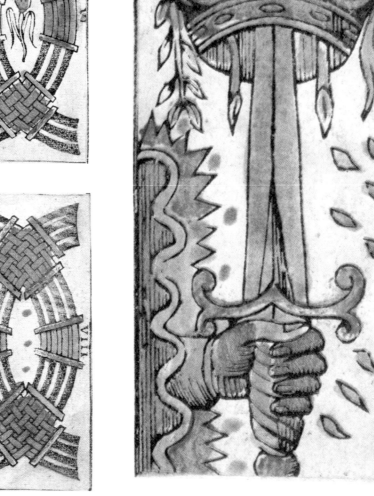
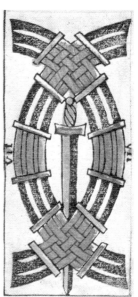
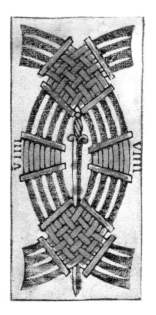

ROY DE DENIERS   ROY DE COVPES   ROY DE SPE   ROY DE BASTONS

CHEVAL DE DENIER   CHEVAL DE COVPES   CHEVAL DE SPE   CHEVAL DE BASTON

VALET DE DENIERS   VALET DE COVPES   VALET DE SPE   VALET DE BASTONS

IL MATTO

IL BAGATTEL.

LA PAPESSA

L'IMPERATRICE

L'IMPERATORE

IL PAPA

GLI AMANTI

IL CARRO

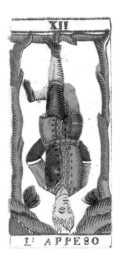

LA GIUSTIZIA

L'EREMITA

RUOT DELLA FOR.

LA FORZA

L'APPESO

717–794 *Gumppenberg Tarot*

XIII

XIX

IL SOLE

XIIII

LA TEMPERAN

XV

IL DIAVOLO

XVI

LA TORRE

XVII

LE STELLE

XVIII

LA LUNA

XX

IL GIUDIZIO

XXI

IL MONDO

FABBRICA DI MILANO

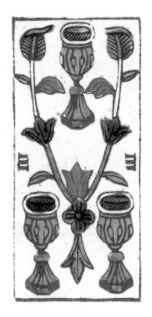

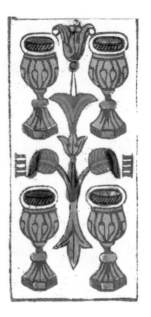

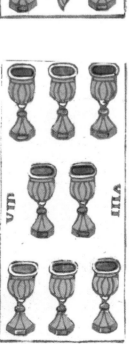

RE DI DANARI   RE DI COPPE   RE DI SPADE   RE DI BASTONI

CAVAL DI DAN   CAVAL DI COPPE   CAVAL DI SPADE   CAV. DI BASTONI

REG. DI DANARI   REG. DI COPPE.   REG. DI SPADE   REG. DI BASTONI

717–794 *Gumppenberg Tarot*